Earth's Changing Land

Beth Geiger

PICTURE CREDITS

Cover, Lonely Planet Images/Getty Images, Inc.; pages 1, 18 (top), 34 (second from bottom), Royalty-Free/Corbis; pages 2-3, Richard Hamilton Smith/Corbis; pages 4 (bottom left), 11 (right), Tom Bean/Corbis; pages 4-5 (top), Owen Franken/Corbis; pages 4-5 (bottom), 10, 22, 25 (top right), 35 (center), David Muench/Corbis; pages 5 (left), 8 (bottom left), 11 (left), 25 (bottom left), 34 (bottom), Taxi/Getty Images; pages 6-7, 35 (bottom), Digital Vision/Getty Images; page 8 (top left), William Manning/Corbis; page 8 (top right), Kate Thompson/National Geographic Image Collection; page 8 (bottom right), Getty Images; pages 9, 25 (top left), 31 (top), 35 (second from top, second from bottom), Photodisc Red/Getty Images; pages 12, 25 (bottom right), 35 (top), Lloyd Cluff/Corbis; pages 14, 30 (bottom right), 31 (center), 34 (top), Stone/Getty Images; pages 15, 34 (center), Nicole Duplaix/National Geographic Image Collection; pages 16-17 (top), 30 (top left), 32, Photodisc Green/Getty Images; pages 16-17 (bottom), 20, 30 (top right), 36, Photographer's Choice/Getty Images; pages 18-19, Pat O'Hara/ Corbis; page 21 (top), Index Stock Imagery/Picture Quest; pages 22-23, LLC, FogStock/Index Stock Imagery; page 26, Associated Press, AP; pages 27, 31 (bottom), Drew Wilson/Virginian Pilot/Corbis Sygma; page 28 (top), Detlev van Ravenswaay/ Photo Researchers, Inc.; page 28 (bottom), Larry Lee Photography/Corbis; page 29 (top), Charles O'Rear/Corbis; page 29 (bottom), Harry Engels/Photo Researchers, Inc.; page 30 (bottom left), George F. Mobley/National Geographic Image Collection; page 34 (second from top), The Image Bank/Getty Images.

Produced through the worldwide resources of the National Geographic Society, John M. Fahey, Jr., President and Chief Executive Officer; Gilbert M. Grosvenor, Chairman of the Board; Nina D. Hoffman, Executive Vice President and President, Books and Education Publishing Group.

PREPARED BY NATIONAL GEOGRAPHIC SCHOOL PUBLISHING

Ericka Markman, Senior Vice President and President, Children's Books and Education Publishing Group; Steve Mico, Senior Vice President, Editorial Director, Publisher; Francis Downey, Executive Editor; Richard Easby, Editorial Manager; Bea Jackson, Director of Layout and Design; Jim Hiscott, Design Manager; Cynthia Olson, Art Director; Margaret Sidlosky, Illustrations Director; Matt Wascavage, Manager of Publishing Services; Sean Philpotts, Jane Ponton, Production Managers; Ted Tucker, Production Specialist.

MANUFACTURING AND QUALITY CONTROL

Christopher A. Liedel, Chief Financial Officer; Phillip L. Schlosser, Director; Clifton M. Brown III, Manager

CONSULTANT AND REVIEWER

Peter Stifel, Professor Emeritus, University of Maryland-College Park

BOOK DEVELOPMENT

Amy Sarver

◄ The lake and islands are landforms.

Contents

BOOK DESIGN/PHOTO RESEARCH
3R1 Group, Inc.

Published by the National Geographic Society
1145 17th Street N.W.
Washington, D.C. 20036-4688

ISBN: 0-7922-5427-9

2014
        6 7 8 9 10 11 12 13 14 15

Printed in Mexico

Landforms A

Landforms are all around you. Landforms are natural features of Earth's surface. You probably know a few kinds of landforms.

Have you ever climbed a hill? Have you gone swimming in a lake? Have you seen a mountain? Hills, lakes, and mountains are all landforms.

Look at the pictures.

- What landforms do you see?
- What kinds of landforms are near where you live?

landform – a natural feature of Earth's surface

lake

e Everywhere!

hill

mountain

Big Idea

Weathering and erosion change the surface of Earth.

Set Purpose

Explore how weathering and erosion shape landforms.

Questions You Will Explore

What causes weathering and erosion?

How can landforms change?

What Changes Landforms?

Landforms do not always stay the same. **Weathering** changes the shape of landforms. Weathering is the wearing away of rocks.

What happens to the rock that wears away? Forces, such as wind and water, move the rock. This is called **erosion**. Erosion is the movement of rock and soil from one place to another.

weathering – the wearing away of rock

erosion – the movement of rock and soil from one place to another

Weathering and erosion change the shape of these landforms.

Forces That Move

Weathering and erosion are caused by natural forces. These forces include:

- wind
- water
- ice
- gravity

These forces wear away rock or move pieces of rock from one place to another.

▼ Weathering and erosion can be caused by wind, water, ice, and gravity.

Forces That Cause Erosion

wind

water

ice

gravity

Water at Work

Moving water can change Earth's surface. Ocean waves and fast-flowing rivers strike against rock. This slowly wears the rock away. Moving water carries the worn rock and drops it in other places.

Water can create landforms. Think of a **valley.** A valley is a landform that can be formed by a river. The river water picks up rock and soil and carries them downstream. Over time, the river wears away enough rock to form a valley.

valley – a low area surrounded by high land, such as hills or mountains

▼ River water helped to form this deep valley.

river

9

Wind Wears Away

Wind can be a powerful force. It can slowly wear away rock. A strong wind can also blow bits of rock and soil from one place to another.

Wind can shape landforms. In a sandy desert, the wind blows the sand into huge hills. These hills are called **sand dunes.**

....

sand dune – a hill of sand

▼ Wind can move sand into hills called sand dunes.

sand dune

Glaciers Erode

Ice can also cause weathering and erosion. **Glaciers** are huge masses of ice. They slowly move over land. Glaciers wear away rock and soil under the ice. Then the glaciers move the rock and soil to another place.

Some glaciers are so large that they can move rocks the size of school buses. Glaciers can also grind away large areas of land. Glaciers can form deep valleys. Sometimes these valleys fill with water and form lakes.

....

glacier – a large mass of ice that moves across land

glacier

▲ A glacier wears away land as it moves between the mountains.

▲ This valley was formed by a glacier long ago.

11

Gravity Pulls Down

Gravity is another force that can change the land. Gravity is the force that pulls objects toward each other. Earth's gravity can pull rock and soil down a hill.

Gravity is a force of erosion. Gravity moves rock and soil from one place to another. Suppose bits of rock are loosened on a hillside. Gravity will cause the rocks to roll to the bottom of the hill.

gravity – the force that pulls objects toward each other

▼ **Gravity pulled this rock and soil down the hill.**

Forces Working Together

Water, wind, ice, and gravity cause weathering and erosion. Most of the time, these forces do not work alone. These forces work together to change landforms. Think of high cliffs by the ocean. Ocean waves hit the land. Strong winds can loosen bits of rock on the cliff. The water and wind wear away the rock. Then gravity causes the rock to fall down. All of these forces work together to change the land.

▼ Wind, water, and gravity work together to shape the cliff.

Forces of Weathering and Erosion

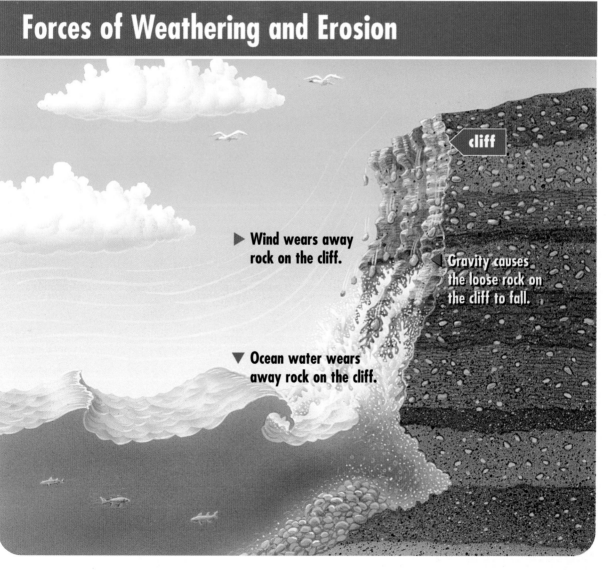

cliff

▶ Wind wears away rock on the cliff.

Gravity causes the loose rock on the cliff to fall.

▼ Ocean water wears away rock on the cliff.

Wearing Down, Building Up

Erosion carries away a lot of rock and soil. What happens to this rock and soil? It is **deposited,** or dropped, in new places. Over time, these bits can create other landforms.

For example, a **delta** is a landform at the mouth of a river. It is low, watery land. A delta forms from the bits of rock and soil deposited by the river.

deposit – to drop

delta – a landform made by the material carried by a river

▼ **This delta formed from bits of rock and soil deposited by the river.**

Small Changes, Big Results

A stream washes away rock. A glacier moves rock and soil. Wind moves sand into sand dunes. These changes may seem small. But the results are big. Weathering and erosion change landforms. They also build new landforms. Over time, weathering and erosion change Earth's surface.

Stop and Think!

What forces change landforms?

▼ **Weathering and erosion shape the rocks at this beach.**

Recap

Explain how water, wind, ice, and gravity change landforms.

Set Purpose

Learn how weathering and erosion have shaped two mountains.

Mounta
High and

ns
ow

Let's go on an adventure! We will hike to the top of two different mountains. One mountain is tall with sharp tops. The other is low with rounded tops. How have weathering and erosion shaped these mountains?

▼ The Appalachian Mountains

Into the Cascades

The Cascade Range is a group of mountains. The mountains are tall and snow-covered. Their peaks, or tops, are pointed. The Cascades are young mountains. They are only about 25 million years old.

We are hiking to a tall mountain called Mount Redoubt in Washington State. **Geologist** Jon Riedel will show us the way. Before we leave, Jon stuffs a lot of gear in his backpack. He says that our adventure will take two days. We will have to hike up more than 1,800 meters (6,000 feet)!

Mount Redoubt

Mount Redoubt

Cascade Range

WASHINGTON

geologist – a scientist who studies rocks

18

glacier

valley

lake

▲ The glacier wears away and erodes the land in this valley.

A Glacier in Action

We start hiking through a valley. A stream rushes below us. The moving water in the stream wears away bits of rock and soil from the valley.

Above us, there is a huge mass of ice. It is Redoubt Glacier. The movement of the glacier wears away the rock on the mountain. It carves this valley. It even eroded the land that is now covered by a lake.

▲ The mountain peaks
are tall and pointed.

Pointed Peaks

The next day, we walk up to Redoubt Glacier.
Then we climb the rocky cliffs. Jon explains
that the winters here are very cold. Ice can
form inside tiny cracks in the rock. This can
make the rock break into bits. Water, wind,
and gravity move these tiny bits of rock.

Finally, we reach the top of Mount Redoubt.
We are nearly 9,000 feet (2,700 meters)
above sea level. It is very cold but the view
is incredible. We see tall, pointed mountains
in every direction.

The Gentle Appalachians

We climbed Mount Redoubt. Yet our journey is not over. We travel to Pennsylvania to visit another mountain. Geologist Francesca Smith will lead us on a hike up Mount Nittany. Mount Nittany is a mountain in the Appalachian Mountains.

After our big Cascade adventure, we are all packed and ready. But Francesca is not carrying a big pack. Instead, she just ties a jacket around her waist. We will be able to climb Mount Nittany in just an afternoon.

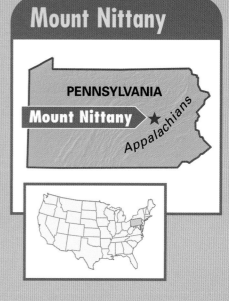

Mount Nittany

PENNSYLVANIA

Mount Nittany

Appalachians

▲ The Appalachian
Mountains are rounded
and low.

Old Mountains

We hike on a trail through the woods. The
Appalachians sure are different from the Cascades.
There are no glaciers. There are no tall peaks.
Instead, the Appalachians are rounded and low.
Mount Nittany is only about 600 meters (2,000
feet) high.

Francesca explains that 225 million years ago,
the Appalachians were higher than the Cascades.
What happened? Weathering and erosion! Water,
wind, and gravity have worn down these
mountains for more than 200 million years.

▲ Many forests and farms cover the Appalachian Mountains.

Green and Rolling

In just an hour, we reach the top of the mountain. There is plenty of room to walk around. Weathering and erosion have made the top of the mountain nearly flat.

Through the trees, we look at the view. Below us, farms fill a wide valley. We can see other low Appalachian mountain tops around us. The smooth and low Appalachian Mountains are very different from the tall and pointed Cascades!

Stop and Think!

HOW have weathering and erosion shaped the Cascade Range and Appalachian Mountains?

Recap
Explain how weathering and erosion can shape mountain ranges.

Set Purpose
Read these articles to learn more about weathering and erosion.

CONNECT WHAT YOU HAVE LEARNED

Landforms Change

Every moment, weathering and erosion change Earth's surface. Many forces cause weathering and erosion.

Here are some ideas you learned about weathering and erosion.

- Water wears away and moves land.
- Wind wears away and moves land.
- Ice wears away and moves land.
- Gravity moves land.

Check What You Have Learned

What do the photos show about weathering and erosion?

▲ River water wears away and moves rock to form this valley.

▲ Sand dunes form when wind wears away and moves sand.

▲ The icy glacier wears away and moves land between the mountains.

▲ Gravity pulls rock and soil down the hill.

A Sinking Landform

Caves are landforms. They are large, underground spaces. Caves can form when water weathers and erodes rock underground. What happens when a cave gets bigger and bigger? The ground over the cave can fall in! The result is a landform called a sinkhole. One day in Winter Park, Florida, a huge sinkhole appeared. It was 27 meters (90 feet) deep. It was wider than a soccer field!

▼ **The sinkhole in Winter Park, Florida, was very wide and deep.**

▲ The Cape Hatteras lighthouse was moved because the beach around it was wearing away.

A Lighthouse on the Move

Weathering and erosion can really get things moving at the beach. At Cape Hatteras, North Carolina, ocean water wore away the sandy beach. So the Cape Hatteras lighthouse had to be moved.

In 1999, the lighthouse was moved to another place along the beach. If it had not been moved, water might have moved the sand below the lighthouse. The lighthouse could have fallen into the ocean.

Meteorite Craters

Once in a while, a chunk of rock from outer space crashes into Earth. A rock from space is called a meteorite. When it hits, a meteorite can make quite a dent in the land. The dent is a type of landform called a crater. One crater in Arizona is more than one kilometer (a half mile) across! The meteorite that made it hit Earth about 50,000 years ago.

meteorite

▶ **This crater in Arizona is deep and wide.**

CONNECT TO ANIMALS

Busy **Beavers**

Animals can create landforms, too. Beavers are some of the best builders in the animal world. They build dams that block streams. These dams can create small lakes. Then the beavers build their homes in the lakes. A beaver dam can be 450 meters (1,500 feet) long!

beaver

◀ **This beaver dam blocks a stream to make a small lake.**

Many kinds of words are used in this book. Here you will learn about antonyms. You will also learn about compound words.

Antonyms

Antonyms are words that have opposite meanings. Find the antonyms below. Then use each antonym in your own sentence.

The peaks of the Cascades are **high.**

The peaks of the Appalachians are **low.**

The wind **erodes** the sand.

Water **deposits** soil in the delta.

Compound Words

Compound words are words made by joining two shorter words. What words are joined to make each compound word? What does each word mean?

land + form = landform

A mountain is a **landform.**

back + pack = backpack

He carries a **backpack.**

light + house = lighthouse

This **lighthouse** was moved.

Write About Weathering and Erosion

Research weathering and erosion. Find out what forces can wear away a sand castle. Keep a journal to record what you learned.

Research

In a large bucket, mix water with sand. On a tray, make a sand castle. Put the sand castle outside.

Observe and Take Notes

Each day, look at the sand castle. Draw what the sand castle looks like.

Write

Write in a journal each day. Tell how the sand castle changed. Explain what forces caused the sand castle to change.

Read More About Weathering and Erosion

Find and read other books about weathering and erosion. As you read, think about these questions.

- What causes weathering and erosion?
- How can weathering and erosion shape land?
- Why do scientists study weathering and erosion?

Books to Read

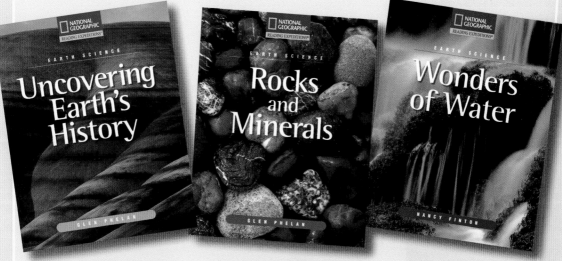

▲ Learn how Earth's land has changed over time.

▲ Read about different kinds of rocks and minerals.

▲ Read about how water shapes land.

Glossary

delta (page 14)
A landform made by the material carried by a river
The water in the river formed the delta.

deposit (page 14)
To drop
These rocks were deposited on the road.

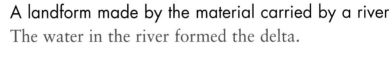

erosion (page 7)
The movement of rock and soil from one place to another
Water can cause erosion.

geologist (page 18)
A scientist who studies rocks
The geologist teaches the hikers about the rocks
on the mountain.

glacier (page 11)
A large mass of ice that moves across land
The glacier moves between the mountains.

gravity (page 12)
The force that pulls objects toward each other
Gravity can move rocks downhill.

landform (page 4)
A natural feature of Earth's surface
This mountain is a landform.

sand dune (page 10)
A hill of sand
Wind moves sand into sand dunes.

valley (page 9)
A low area surrounded by high land, such as hills
or mountains
A river runs through this valley.

weathering (page 7)
The wearing away of rock
Weathering can change the shape of a landform.

Index